I CAN'T BELIEVE YOU SAID THAT!

I CAN'T BELIEVE YOU SAID THAT!

A Second Book of Insults

Compiled by:
William Cole and
Louis Phillips

St. Martin's Press
New York

Production Editor: David Stanford Burr

Design: Junie Lee

Library of Congress Cataloging-in-Publication Data

I can't believe you said that! / William Cole and Louis
    Phillips, editors.
            p.   cm.
        "A Thomas Dunne book."
        ISBN 0-312-10479-0
        1. Invective—Humor.   2. Celebrities—Humor.
    I. Cole, William, 1919–
    II. Phillips, Louis.
    PN6231.I65I2   1994
    081—dc20   93-45285
                                                    CIP

First Edition: April 1994

10   9   8   7   6   5   4   3   2   1

Insult begets insult as bugs beget bugs.

—American Proverb

The only gracious way to accept an insult is to ignore it; if you can't ignore it, top it; if you can't top it, laugh at it; if you can't laugh at it, it's probably deserved.

—Russell Lynes

"He called me a muddleheaded old ass," he said. "Well, you are a muddleheaded old ass," I pointed out, quick as a flash, and he seemed to see the justice of this.

—P. G. Wodehouse

PRESIDENT JOHN ADAMS

It has been the political career of this man to begin with hypocrisy, proceed with arrogance, and finish with contempt.

—Tom Paine

JACK ANDERSON

. . . he'll go lower than dogshit for a story.

—J. Edgar Hoover

BENEDICT ARNOLD

From some traits of his character which have lately come to my knowledge, he seems to have been so hackneyed in villainy and so lost to all sense of honor and shame that while his facilities will enable him to continue his sordid pursuits there will be no time for remorse.

—President George Washington

MATTHEW ARNOLD

Poor Matt, he's gone to Heaven, no doubt—
but he won't like God.

> —Robert Louis Stevenson

CLEMENT ATTLEE

Mr. Attlee touches nothing that he does not
dehydrate.

> —*The Economist*

LOUIS AUCHINCLOSS

He's a second-rate Stephen Birmingham.
And Stephen Birmingham is third-rate.

> —Truman Capote

W. H. AUDEN

. . . a sort of gutless Kipling.

> —George Orwell

JANE AUSTEN

Jane Austen's books, too, are absent from this library. Just that one omission alone would make a fairly good library out of a library that hadn't a book in it.

—Mark Twain

She was then the prettiest, silliest, most affected, husband-hunting butterfly she ever remembers.

—Mary Russell Mitford

SIR FRANCIS BACON

When their lordships asked Bacon
How many bribes he had taken
He had at least the grace
To get very red in the face.

—Edmund Clerihew Bentley

BOBBY BAKER, FRIEND OF AMERICAN PRESIDENTS

As for Bobby Baker, we have a new measure in Washington. It's called the Baker's dozen. They give you thirteen and you kick back two.

—Barry Goldwater

ARTHUR BALFOUR

His impact on history would be no more than the whiff of scent on a lady's handkerchief.

—David Lloyd George

TALLULAH BANKHEAD

Queen of the Nil.

—George Jean Nathan

THEDA BARA

She was divinely, hysterically, insanely malevolent.

—Bette Davis

ROSEANNE BARR

The closest thing to Roseanne Barr's singing the national anthem was my cat being neutered.

—Johnny Carson

JOHN BARTH

Whatever Professor Barth's gifts, humor, irony, wit are entirely lacking from his ambitious, garrulous, jocose productions.

—Gore Vidal

BELA BARTOK

If the reader were so rash to purchase any of Bela Bartok's compositions, he would find that they each and all consist of an unmeaning bunch of notes, apparently representing the composer promenading the keyboard in his boots.

—Frederick Corder

Aubrey Beardsley

A monstrous orchid.

—Oscar Wilde

Lord Beaverbrook

Beaverbrook is so pleased to be in the government that he is like the town tart who has finally married the mayor.

—Beverly Baxter

Samuel Beckett

[his plays] remind me of something Sir John Betjeman might do if you filled him up with benzedrine and then force-fed him Guinness intravenously.

—Tom Davis

Max Beerbohm

Tell me, when you are alone with Max, does he take off his face and reveal his mask?

—Oscar Wilde

SAUL BELLOW

The results of American literary elephantiasis can be seen in such curiousities as Saul Bellow's reputation.

—Kingsley Amis

ANTHONY WEDGWOOD BENN, BRITISH POLITICIAN

I have always said about Tony that he immatures with age.

—Harold Wilson

Benn flung himself into the sixties technology with the enthusiasm (not to say language) of a newly enrolled Boy Scout demonstrating knot-tying to his indulgent parents.

—Bernard Levin

JAMES GORDON BENNETT, EDITOR OF THE *NEW YORK HERALD*

A reptile marking his path with slime wherever he goes, and breathing a mildew at everything fresh and fragrant; a midnight ghoul, preying on rottenness and repulsive filth; a creature, hated by his nearest intimates, and bearing the consciousness thereof upon his distorted features, and upon his despicable soul; one whom men avoid as a blot to his nature—whom all despise, and whom no one blesses—all this is James Gordon Bennett.

—Walt Whitman

CHARLES, LORD BERESFORD

When my right honorable friend Lord Charles rose to his feet, he had not the least idea what he was going to say. Moreover, he did not know what he was saying when he was speaking. And when he sat down, he was doubtless unable to remember what he had said.

—Sir Winston Churchill

SARAH BERNHARDT

A great actress from the waist down.

—Dame Margaret Kendal

ANEURIN BEVAN, FOUNDER OF THE NATIONAL HEALTH SERVICE

I can think of no better step to signalize the inauguration of the National Health Service than that a person who so obviously needs psychiatric attention should be among the first of its patients.

—Sir Winston Churchill
(1948)

A merchant of discourtesy.

—Sir Winston Churchill

SENATOR THEODORE BILBO

When Bilbo dies, the epitaph on his grave-stone should read:
Here lies Bilbo, deep in the dirt he loved so well.

—Senator Pat Harrison

BILLY THE KID (WILLIAM BONNEY)

A nondescript, adenoidal, weasel-eyed, narrow-chested, stoop-shouldered, repulsive creature with all the outward appearance of a cretin.

—Burton Rascoe

JAMES G. BLAINE, AMERICAN POLITICIAN

Wallowing in corruption like a rhinoceros in an African pool.

—E. L. Godkin

NAPOLEON BONAPARTE

That infernal creature who is the curse of all the human race becomes every day more and more abominable.

—Alexander I of Russia

SIR ALFRED BOSSOM

Bossom? What an extraordinary name. Neither one thing nor the other!

—Sir Winston Churchill

JAMES BOSWELL

Servile and impertinent, shallow and pedantic, a bigot and a sot, bloated with family pride, and eternally blustering about the dignity of a born gentleman, yet stooping to be a talebearer, an eavesdropper, a common butt in the taverns of London. . . . Everything which another man would have hidden, everything the publication of which would have made another man hang himself, was a matter of exaltation to his weak and diseased mind.

—Thomas Babington Macaulay

CHARLES BOYER

I am *not* some delicate female who droops. That "old lady" Boyer does that enough for everybody.

—Marlene Dietrich
(when the press reported that
she had fainted on the set)

JOHANNES BRAHMS

Art is long and life is short; here is evidently the explanation of a Brahms symphony.

—Edward Lorne

LEONID BREZHNEV

Shit floats.

—Nikita Kruschev
(on Brezhnev's rise to the top)

LOUISE BROOKS

If I ever write a part for a cigar store Indian, she'd get it.

—Anita Loos

ROBERT BROWNING

His verse . . . is the beads without the string.

—Gerard Manley Hopkins

ANTON BRUCKNER

Anton Bruckner wrote the same symphony nine times (ten, actually), trying to get it just right. He failed.

—Edward Abbey

WILLIAM JENNINGS BRYAN

The president of the United States may be an ass, but at least he doesn't believe that the earth is square, and that witches should be put to death, and that Jonah swallowed the whale.

—H. L. Mencken

His mind was like a soup dish: wide and shallow. It could hold a small amount of nearly anything, but the slightest jarring spilled the soup into somebody's lap.

—Irving Stone

PATRICK BUCHANAN

If George Bush reminds many women of their first husbands, Pat Buchanan reminds women why an increasing number of them are staying single.

—Judy Pearson

WILLIAM F. BUCKLEY, JR.

I think Buckley's a fool who spends too much time caressing dictionaries. Remember when he and Gore Vidal were at the Democratic convention and Vidal called Buckley a crypto-Nazi and Buckley called Vidal a faggot. That's American politics in a nutshell, folks. These are our commentators.

—Ian Shoales

Over the years, if there is any false witness to be borne, William F. Buckley, Jr., can usually be counted on to shoulder the burden.

—Gore Vidal

PRESIDENT GEORGE BUSH

Where I part company with my contemporary from Kennebunkport, Texas, is that he has no known political principles or even opinions other than how to master the stage business necessary for him to take the temporary lead in a play he knows by heart but has not, perhaps, taken to heart.

—Gore Vidal

George Bush has a much more visible absence than Ronald Reagan.

—Lance Morrow

. . . a toothache of a man.

—Jim Hightower
(radio commentator)

George Bush is Gerald Ford without the pizzazz.

—Pat Paulsen

A cross between Rambo and Mary Poppins.

—Peter Fenn

Poor George, he can't help it—he was born with a silver foot in his mouth.

—Ann Richards

Every woman's first husband.
                    Barbara Ehrenreich and Jane O'Reilly

GEORGE GORDON, LORD BYRON

I hate the whole race of them, there never existed a more worthless set than Byron and his friends.

—Duke of Wellington

The world is rid of Lord Byron, but the deadly slime of his touch still remains.

—John Constable

A coxcomb who would have gone into hysterics if a tailor had laughed at him.
—Ebenezer Elliott

MRS. PATRICK CAMPBELL, ENGLISH ACTRESS

An ego like a raging tooth.
—William Butler Yeats

TRUMAN CAPOTE

He'd be all right if he took his finger out of his mouth.
—Harold Robbins

. . . wears with a certain panache the boa of the late Louella Parsons.
—Gore Vidal

ELLIOTT CARTER

I would like to hear Elliott Carter's *Fourth String Quartet,* if only to discover what a cranky prostate does to one's polyphony.
—James Sellars

PRESIDENT JIMMY CARTER

Don't let Jimmy Carter pull the peanut butter over your eyes.

—Julian Bond

Jimmy Carter had the air of a man who had never taken any decisions in his life. They had always taken him.

—Guy Simon

NEVILLE CHAMBERLAIN

Look at his head. The worst thing Neville Chamberlain ever did was to meet Hitler and let Hitler see him.

—David Lloyd George

The worst thing I can say about democracy is that it has tolerated the Right Honorable Gentleman for four and a half years.

—Aneurin Bevan

In the depths of that dusty soul there is nothing but abject surrender.

—Sir Winston Churchill

He saw foreign policy through the wrong end of a municipal drainpipe.
—David Lloyd George

LORD CHESTERFIELD

They [his letters] teach the morals of a whore, and the manners of a dancing master.
—Samuel Johnson

G. K. CHESTERTON

He grew up from manhood into boyhood.
—R. A. Knox

RICHARD CHURCH, ENGLISH LITERARY MAN

. . . a cliché-ridden humbug and pie-fingering hack.

—Dylan Thomas

RANDOLPH CHURCHILL

No one who knows Mr. Randolph Churchill and wishes to express distaste for him should ever be at a loss for words which would be both opprobrious and apt.

—Evelyn Waugh

SIR WINSTON CHURCHILL

Churchill has the habit of breaking the rungs of any ladder he puts his foot on.

—Lord Beaverbrook

HENRY CLAY, AMERICAN STATESMAN

He was a chameleon; he could turn any color that might be useful to him. To read of his career one must have corkscrew eyes.

—Irving Stone

I have only two regrets: that I have not shot
Henry Clay or hanged John C. Calhoun.
—Andrew Jackson

PRESIDENT GROVER CLEVELAND

Harrison is a wise man,
        Cleveland is a fool;
Harrison rides a white horse
        Cleveland rides a mule.

—Campaign song
(1892)

BILL CLINTON AND AL GORE

My dog Millie knows more about foreign
policy than those two bozos.

—George Bush

HARRY COHN

He liked to be the biggest bug in the
manure pile.

—Elia Kazan

SAMUEL TAYLOR COLERIDGE

Coleridge was a muddleheaded metaphysician who by some strange streak of fortune turned out a few poems amongst the dreary flood of inanity that was his wont.

—William Morris

JOHN CONNALLY

John Connally's conversion to the GOP raised the intellectual level of both parties.

—Frank Mankiewicz

JOSEPH CONRAD

What is Conrad but the wreck of Stevenson floating about in the slipslop of Henry James?

—George Moore

I cannot abide Conrad's souvenir-shop style, and bottled ships and shell necklaces or romanticist clichés.

—Vladimir Nabokov

CALVIN COOLIDGE

. . . this runty, aloof, little man, who quacks through his nose when he speaks.

—William Allen White

I think the American people want a solemn ass as a president. I think I'll go along with them.

—Coolidge
(on himself)

The vacuum in the White House.

—H. L. Mencken

HOWARD COSELL, AMERICAN SPORTS BROADCASTER

"Tell it like it is!" says Howard Cosell, self-appointed purveyor of honesty. So why does he wear a toupee?

—Edwin Miller

JOAN CRAWFORD

Toward the end of her life she looked like a hungry insect magnified a million times—a praying mantis that had forgotten how to pray.

—Quentin Crisp

SIR STAFFORD CRIPPS

Sir Stafford has built a high stone wall around his mind, as though it were an intellectual nudist colony.

—*Tribune*

ALEISTER CROWLEY

. . . one of the most depraved, vicious, and revolting humbugs who ever escaped from a nightmare or a lunatic asylum.

—Preston Sturges

GEORGE NATHANIEL CURZON, STATESMAN

I met Curzon in Downing Street, from whom I got the sort of greeting a corpse would give to an undertaker.

—Stanley Baldwin

TYNE DALY, AMERICAN ACTRESS

Shaped like a sack of potatoes left out in the rain, gifted with a mouth that cries out for some cud to chew on, and sounding like a Brooklyn policewoman on a beloved TV series, Miss Daly throws her not inconsiderable weight about hither and yon, only to land with unerring precision on the line or situation she deems in need of crushing.

—John Simon

SALVADOR DALI

AVIDA DOLLARS

—André Breton
(an anagram)

John Davenport, English literary critic

You never knew where you were with Davenport; worse, you did not quite know where Davenport was, if anywhere. . . .

—Geoffrey Grigson

Charles de Gaulle

An improbable creature, like a human giraffe, sniffing down his nostril at mortals beneath his gaze.

—Richard Wilson

. . . just an old man who went to South America and fell on his ass.

—Lyndon B. Johnson

SANDY DENNIS

Pauline Kael has aptly observed that Miss Dennis "has made an acting style out of postnasal drip." It should be added that she balanced her postnasal condition with something like prefrontal lobotomy, so that when she is not a walking catarrh she is a blithering imbecile.

—John Simon

BERNARD DE VOTO

I denounce Mr. Bernard De Voto as a fool and a tedious and egotistical fool, as a liar and a pompous and boresome liar.

—Sinclair Lewis

THOMAS E. DEWEY, U.S. PRESIDENTIAL CANDIDATE

I know Governor Thomas E. Dewey and Mr. Dewey is a fine man. So is my Uncle Morris. My Uncle Morris shouldn't be president, neither should Dewey.

—George Jessel

He is small and insignificant, and he makes too much of an effort, with his forced smile and jovial manner, to impress himself upon people. To me he is a political streetwalker accosting men with "come home with me, dear."

—Harold Ickes

He is just about the nastiest little man I've ever known. He struts sitting down.

—Mrs. Dykstra
(quoted in book *Mr. Republican*)

JOAN DIDION

Ask her how come, if she spends all her time crying and swimming and struggling to open a car door, she finds the energy to write so much?

—Gloria Steinem
(to journalist about to interview Didion)

BENJAMIN DISRAELI

He is a self-made man and worships his creator.

—John Bright
(attributed)

He fancies himself young . . . his soul wears a turned-down collar; it eats lollipops at school.

—William Makepeace Thackeray

HELEN GAHAGAN DOUGLAS, POLITICAL OPPONENT OF NIXON

. . . pink down to her underwear.

—Richard M. Nixon

KIRK DOUGLAS

I suppose he looks all right, if your tastes happen to run to septuagenarians with blow waves and funny stretch marks around the ears.

—Lynn Barker

STEPHEN A. DOUGLAS

. . . I did keep a grocery, and I did sell cotton, candles, and cigars, and sometimes whiskey; but I remember in those days Mr. Douglas was one of my best customers. Many a time have I stood on one side of the

counter and sold whiskey to Mr. Douglas
on the other side, but the difference
between us now is this: I have left my side
of the counter, but Mr. Douglas still sticks to
his tenaciously as ever.

—Abraham Lincoln

THEODORE DREISER

A natural-born cheap bastard, actively dishonest whenever he got an opportunity to be; stupidly and grossly undiscerning whenever discernment was called for; and voluminous producer of perhaps the worst English prose that ever found itself printed and bound in books.

—James Gould Cozzens

JOHN DRYDEN

His imagination resembles the wings of an ostrich.

—Thomas Babington Macaulay

JOHN FOSTER DULLES, AMERICAN STATESMAN

The world's longest range misguided missile.

—Walter Reuther
(attributed)

LAWRENCE DURRELL

All the old boy's books crumbled on the shelves when the old boy died.

—Seamus Heaney

NELSON EDDY AND JEANETTE MacDONALD

Rub these two sticks together and you won't get a single spark.

—William Cole

ANTHONY EDEN

The best advertisement the fifty-shilling tailors ever had.

—Bonar Thompson

KING EDWARD VII OF ENGLAND

Bertie has remarkable social talent. He is lively, quick, and sharp when his mind is set on anything, which is seldom. . . . But usually his intellect is of no more use than a pistol packed in the bottom of a trunk if one were attacked in the robber-infested Apennines.

—Prince Albert
(his father)

JONATHAN EDWARDS

He believed in the worst God, preached the worst sermons, and had the worst religion of any human being who ever lived on this continent.

—M. M. Richter

PRESIDENT DWIGHT DAVID EISENHOWER

The incredible dullness wrecked upon the American landscape in Eisenhower's eight years has been a triumph of the corporation. A tasteless, sexless, odorless sanctity in architecture, manners, modes, styles has been the result. Eisenhower embodied half the needs of the nation, the needs of the timid, the petrified, the sanctimonious, and the sluggish.

—Norman Mailer

As an intellectual he bestowed upon the games of golf and bridge all the enthusiasm and perseverance that he withheld from books and ideas.

—Emmet John Hughes

GEORGE ELIOT

. . . a fungus of pendulous shape.

—Alice James

T. S. ELIOT

Both T. S. Eliot and I like to play, but I like to play euchre, while he likes to play Eucharist.

—Robert Frost

QUEEN ELIZABETH I OF ENGLAND

As just and merciful as Nero and as good a Christian as Muhammad.

—John Wesley

QUEEN ELIZABETH II OF ENGLAND

All she requires is sufficiently powerful reading spectacles to be able to drone through her speeches written for her by the prime minister.

—A. N. Wilson

FRANCES FARMER

The nicest thing I can say about Frances Farmer is that she is unbearable.

—William Wyler

WILLIAM FAULKNER

I knew Faulkner very well. He was a great friend of mine. Well, much as you could be a friend of his, unless you were a fourteen-year-old nymphet.

—Truman Capote

IAN FLEMING

When he greeted one, one always felt like a delicate monkey being put through tricks.

—Cyril Connolly

ERROL FLYNN

The great thing about Errol was that you knew precisely where you were with him—because he always let you down.

—David Niven

FERDINAND FOCH

. . . only a frantic pair of moustaches.

—T. E. Lawrence

MICHAEL FOOT

. . . the ghost of an old left-winger coming back and desecrating his own grave.

—Anthony Wedgwood Benn

SAMUEL FOOTE

If he is an infidel, he is an infidel as a dog is an infidel; that is to say, he has no thought upon the subject.

—Samuel Johnson

FORD MADOX FORD

. . . a flabby lemon and pink giant, who hung his mouth open as though he were an animal at the zoo inviting buns—especially when ladies were present.

—Wyndham Lewis

... stout, gangling, albinoish ... an embrace from him made you feel like being the toast under a poached egg.

—Rebecca West

GERALD FORD

It troubles me that he played center on the football team. That means he can only consider options for the twenty yards in either direction, and that he has spent a good deal of his life looking at the world upside down through his legs.

—Martin Perez

He looks and talks like he just fell off Edgar Bergen's lap.

—David Steinberg

I've never met him, but I used to spend time in Ohio, and they turn out Jerry Fords by the bale.

—Alice Roosevelt Longworth

BENJAMIN FRANKLIN

. . . is a crafty and lecherous old hypocrite . . . whose very statue seems to gloat on the wenches as they walk the State House yard.

—William Cobbett

SIGMUND FREUD

Nobody can read Freud without realizing that he was the scientific equivalent of another nuisance, George Bernard Shaw.

—Robert Maynard Hutchins

ROBERT FROST

For him, as he liked to say, there was room for only one at the top of the steeple; he demanded to be the one. He was jealous of all other poets.

—Donald Hall

If it were thought that anything I wrote was influenced by Robert Frost, I would take that particular work of mine, shred it, and flush it down the toilet, hoping not to clog the pipes. A more sententious, holding-forth old bore who expected every hero-worshipping adenoidal little twerp of a student-poet to hang on his every word I never saw.

—James Dickey

DAVID PATRICK MAXWELL FYFE

The nearest thing to death in life
Is David Patrick Maxwell Fyfe,
Though underneath that gloomy shell
He does himself extremely well.

—E. Grierson

ZSA ZSA GABOR

. . . the only person who ever left the Iron Curtain wearing it.

—Oscar Levant

MAHATMA GANDHI

You've no idea what it costs to keep the old man in poverty.

—Lord Mountbatten

[it is] alarming and also nauseating to see Mr. Gandhi, a seditious Middle Temple lawyer, now posing as a fakir well-known in the east, striding half-naked up the steps of the vice-regal palace.

—Sir Winston Churchill

DAVID GARRICK

On the stage he was natural, simple, affecting;
'Twas only that when he was off he was
acting.

—Oliver Goldsmith

KING GEORGE I OF ENGLAND

In private life he would have been called an
honest blockhead.

—Lady Mary Wortley Montagu

LILLIAN GISH

. . . poor, dried-up, bent-shouldered, flat-
voiced, peanut-headed little chicken, the
ideal of the haberdashery clerk and of all
other chumps who never heard of Rubens
or the Greeks or fresh air.

—Ralph Barton
(1914)

WILLIAM GLADSTONE

A sophisticated rhetorician, inebriated with the exuberance of his own verbosity, and gifted with an egotistical imagination that can at all times command interminable and inconsistent series of arguments, malign an opponent and glorify himself.

> —Benjamin Disraeli
> (in parody of the prime minister's oratory)

JACKIE GLEASON

The worst person I ever worked with in forty years in show business.

> —Gene Wolsk
> (theatrical manager)

HERBERT GOLD, AMERICAN NOVELIST

Herbert Gold used to be a mosquito. Now he is an angry mosquito. I better get my ass covered.

> —Norman Mailer

ALBERT GOLDMAN, ROCK MUSIC CRITIC AND BIOGRAPHER

World's Oldest Rock Hack and one of the worst . . . a pompous airhead and a prick as well.

—John Strausbaugh

OLIVER GOLDSMITH

The misfortune of Goldsmith in conversation is this: He goes on without knowing how he is going to get off.

—Samuel Johnson

It is amazing how little Goldsmith knows. He seldom comes where he is not more ignorant than anyone else.

—Samuel Johnson

BARRY GOLDWATER

I don't care if you study ancient history, but don't vote for it.

—Hubert Humphrey

The Catskills were immortalized by Washington Irving. He wrote of a man who fell asleep and awoke in another era. The only other area that can boast such a man is Phoenix, Arizona.

—Robert F. Kennedy

Why, this man Goldwater is living so far in the past and is so handsome that he was offered a movie contract by Eighteenth Century-Fox.

—Hubert Humphrey

SAMUEL GOLDWYN

You always knew where you were with Goldwyn. Nowhere.

—F. Scott Fitzgerald

THOMAS GRAY

Sir, he was dull in company, dull in his closet, dull everywhere. He was dull in a new way, and that made people think him great.

—Samuel Johnson

JOYCE HABER, GOSSIP COLUMNIST

They should give Haber open-heart surgery—
and go in through the feet.

—Julie Andrews

ARTHUR HAILEY

When book buyers buy books, they look for
sex, violence, and hard information. They
get these from Arthur Hailey, whose char-
acters discuss problems of hotel manage-
ment while committing adultery before
being beaten up.

—Anthony Burgess

PRESIDENT WARREN G. HARDING

. . . a platitudinous jellyfish . . . a man upon
whom the Lord conferred a bunch of wet
spaghetti instead of a backbone.

—Harold L. Ickes

FRANK HARRIS

Frank Harris is not second-rate, nor third-rate nor fifth. He is just his own horrible self.

—George Bernard Shaw

PRESIDENT BENJAMIN HARRISON

He is a cold-blooded, narrow-minded, prejudiced, obstinate, timid old psalm-singing Indianapolis politician.

—Theodore Roosevelt

WILLIAM HAZLITT

His manners are ninety-nine in a hundred singularly repulsive.

—Samuel Taylor Coleridge

He is not a proper person to be admitted into respectable society, being the most perverse and malevolent creature that ill luck has thrown my way.

—William Wordsworth

ERNEST HEMINGWAY

Always willing to lend a hand to the one above him.

—F. Scott Fitzgerald

A literary style . . . of wearing false hair on the chest.

—Max Eastman

I read him for the first time in the early forties, something about bells, balls, and bulls, and loathed it.

—Vladimir Nabokov

. . . too bad so indisputable a talent for writing should have had to go with thinking so callow and childish and feeling so often cheap and silly.

—James Gould Cozzens

ERNEST HEMINGWAY AND JOSEPH CONRAD

. . . writers of books for boys.

—Vladimir Nabokov

KING HENRY IV OF ENGLAND

Henry IV's feet and armpits enjoyed an international reputation.

—Aldous Huxley

KING HENRY VIII OF ENGLAND

The plain truth is, that he was a most intolerable ruffian, a disgrace to human nature, and a blot of blood and grease upon the history of England.

—Charles Dickens

HAROLD HOBSON, ENGLISH THEATER CRITIC

One of the most characteristic sounds of the English Sunday morning is the critic Harold Hobson barking up the wrong tree.

—Penelope Gilliat

ERIC HOFFER, AMERICAN POPULAR PHILOSOPHER

Hoffer, our resident Peasant Philosopher, is an example of articulate ignorance.

—John Seelye

PRESIDENT HERBERT HOOVER

A private meeting with Hoover is like sitting in a bath of ink.

—Henry Stimson

Mellon pulled the whistle,
    Hoover rang the bell,
Wall Street gave the signal
    And the country went to hell.

—Campaign jingle during the 1930s

Thomas Hoving, former director of the Metropolitan Museum of Art

. . . a man who could make hay in a down-pour.

—John L. Hess

Hubert Humphrey

All that Hubert needs over there is a gal to answer the phone and a pencil with an eraser on it.

—Lyndon B. Johnson

Saddam Hussein

He is neither a strategist, nor is he schooled in the operational art, nor is he a tactician, nor is he a general, nor is he a soldier. Other than that, he's a great military man.

—General Norman Schwartzkopf

JOHN HUSTON

Figuratively speaking, he left his friends' bodies strewn all over the world.

—Lauren Bacall

HENRIK IBSEN

A crazy fanatic . . . a crazy, cranky being . . . not only consistently dirty but deplorably dull.

—*Truth*
(magazine)

Ugly, nasty, discordant, and downright dull, a gloomy sort of ghoul, bent on groping for horror by night, and blinking like a stupid old owl when the warm sunlight of the best of life dances into his wrinkled eyes.

—*The Gentlewoman*
(magazine)

JEREMY IRONS

. . . he seems ruthless, arrogant, and generally contemptuous of other people.

—Lynn Barber

President Andrew Jackson

I cannot believe that the killing of two thousand Englishmen at New Orleans qualifies a person for the various difficult and complicated duties of the presidency.

—Henry Clay

Glenda Jackson

Has the look of an asexual harlequin.

—John Simon

Glenda Jackson has a face to launch a thousand dredges.

—Jack De Manio

Jesse Jackson

Jesse Jackson is a man of the cloth. Cashmere.

—Mort Sahl

HENRY JAMES

[A novel by Henry James] is like a church lit but without a congregation to distract you, with every light and line focused on the high altar. And on the altar, very reverently placed, intensely there, is a dead kitten, an eggshell, a bit of string.

—H. G. Wells

Henry James has a mind—a sensibility—so fine that no mere idea could ever penetrate it.

—T. S. Eliot

Henry James had turned his back on one of the great events of the world's history, the rise of the United States, in order to report tittle-tattle at tea parties in English country houses.

—W. Somerset Maugham

JOHN JAY, AMERICAN JURIST

Damn John Jay! Damn every one who won't damn John Jay! Damn every one that won't put lights in his windows and sit up all night damning John Jay!!!

—Anonymous

SIR RICHARD CLAVERHOUSE JEBB, GREEK SCHOLAR

It was commonly said, though I do not vouch for the story, that Henry Sidgwick remarked concerning Jebb, "All the time that he can spare from the adornment of his person, he devotes to the neglect of his duties."

—Bertrand Russell

ROBINSON JEFFERS

What an ass that man is! Him and his Pacific Ocean!

—Louise Bogan

PRESIDENT THOMAS JEFFERSON

Should the infidel Jefferson be elected to the presidency, the seal of death is that moment set on our holy religion, our churches will be prostrated, and some infamous prostitute, under the title of goddess of reason, will preside in the sanctuaries now devoted to the worship of the most High.

—*New England Palladium* (1800)

... perhaps the most incapable executive that ever filled the presidential chair. ... It would be difficult to imagine a man less fit to guide a state with honor and safety through the stormy times that marked the opening of the present century.

—Theodore Roosevelt
(1882)

PRESIDENT LYNDON B. JOHNSON

The trouble with Lyndon is that he is a son of a bitch. The next-worst trouble is that he is a great son of a bitch. He will probably do more for the U.S., destroying everyone around him, than any other president.

—an anonymous old friend

You know when I first thought I might have a chance? When I realized that I could go into any bar in this country and insult Lyndon Johnson and nobody would punch you in the nose.

—Eugene McCarthy

PAUL JOHNSON, ENGLISH HISTORIAN AND CONTROVERSIALIST

[He looks like] an explosion in a pubic hair factory.

—Jonathan Miller

JAMES JONES

If you read James Jones long enough, you'll be ashamed to be sober and out of jail.

—Edmund Fuller

BEN JONSON

Reading him is like wading through glue.

—Alfred, Lord Tennyson

HAMILTON JORDAN, PRESIDENTIAL PRESS SECRETARY

I would not piss down Hamilton Jordan's throat if his heart was on fire.

—James Carville
(Bill Clinton advisor)

JAMES JOYCE

The work of a queasy undergraduate scratching his pimples.

—Virginia Woolf
(on *Ulysses*)

Joyce can do no more than thinly veil his banal writing by inverting his sentences and cataloguing old names which he does not know how to use. Lawrence was clean compared with Joyce, who has the miserable lust for the repulsive found in the lower middle classes.

—Edward Dahlberg

. . . just stewed up fragments of quotation in the sauce of a would-be dirty mind.

—D. H. Lawrence

CAROL KANE

You have to have a stomach for ugliness to endure Carol Kane—to say nothing of the zombielike expressions she mistakes for acting.

—John Simon

EDWARD F. KENNEDY

He would have made a very good bartender.

—Gore Vidal

He'll be able to do something this week he's never been able to do before—check into a hotel under his own name.

—Jay Leno
(on Kennedy's honeymoon, 1992)

I admire Ted Kennedy. How many fifty-nine-year-olds do you know who still go to Florida for spring break?

—Patrick Buchanan

PRESIDENT JOHN F. KENNEDY

He was exceedingly vain, incredibly foul-mouthed, petty, penurious, insensitive, spiteful, eager for salacious gossip, and extremely manipulative. He slipped secret government documents to journalists in return for favors, got drunk, favored abortion, and denigrated liberals.

—Ben Bradlee

. . . the only music Jack liked was "Hail to the Chief."

—Jacqueline Kennedy
(attributed)

I sincerely fear for my country if Jack Kennedy should be elected president. The fellow has absolutely no principles. Money and gall are all the Kennedys have.

—Barry Goldwater

JOSEPH P. KENNEDY, FATHER OF PRESIDENT JOHN F. KENNEDY

. . . a loathsome ogre, a crook, a draft dodger and a lecher.

—Nigel Hamilton
(author, *J.F.K. Reckless Youth*)

ROBERT F. KENNEDY

LBJ always referred to Robert Kennedy in one way. He called him "the little shit." I'll buy that in spades although in that connection I wouldn't have called him "little."

—Jimmy Hoffa

FRANK KERMODE, ENGLISH LITERARY MAN

. . . a jumped-up book-drunk ponce.

—Philip Larkin

MARTIN LUTHER KING

Martin Luther King is the most notorious liar in the country.

—J. Edgar Hoover

NEIL KINNOCK

. . . like processed cheese coming out of a mincing machine.

—Anthony Wedgwood Benn
(on his interviews)

HENRY KISSINGER

Kissinger won a Nobel Prize for watching a war end that he was for.

—Eugene McCarthy

[He] became the nation's top foreign-policy strategist despite being born with the handicaps of a laughable accent and no morals or neck.

—Dave Barry

Kissinger is a disaster. His priorities are: one, Kissinger; two, the president; three, the U.S.

—Ghershon Shafat

EDWARD KOCH, MAYOR OF NEW YORK CITY

He has bullied the ill-fortuned and truckled to the fortuned. To walk in his wake has been to stumble through a rubble of vulgarities and meanness of spirit.

—Murray Kempton

JACQUES LACAN, FRENCH PHILOSOPHER

. . . the French fog machine, a gray-flannel worry-bone for toothless academic pups; a twerpy cape-twirling Dracula dragging his flocking stooges to the crypt.

—Camille Paglia

ALAN LADD

Alan Ladd had only two expressions: hat on and hat off.

—Anonymous

Ring Lardner

He looked like Ramses II with his wrappings off.

—Hugh Fullerton

Charles Laughton

He had a face that faintly resembled a large wad of cotton wool.

—Josef von Sternberg

What do you know about men, you fat, ugly faggot?

—Henry Fonda
(during rehearsals of *The Caine Mutiny Court Martial*)

is . . . always hovering somewhere, waiting to be offended.

—Peter Ustinov

ANDREW BONAR LAW, BRITISH PRIME MINISTER

It is fitting that we should have buried the Unknown Prime Minister by the side of the Unknown Soldier.

—Herbert Henry Asquith

D. H. LAWRENCE

He's impossible. He's pathetic and preposterous. He writes like a sick man.

—Gertrude Stein

To my mind his view was the view of a sick man of abnormal irritability, whose nature was warped by poverty and cankered with a rambling envy.

—W. Somerset Maugham

[. . . looked] like a plaster gnome on a stone toadstool in some suburban garden.

—Edith Sitwell

. . . a bloodthirsty fascist with a profound contempt for mankind.

—Bertrand Russell

T. E. LAWRENCE

. . . a bore and a bounder and a prig. He was intoxicated with his own youth, and loathed any milieu which he couldn't dominate. Certainly he had none of a gentleman's instincts, strutting about peace conferences in Arab dress.

—Sir Henry "Chips" Channon

LE CORBUSIER

An artist should put no value on money as money. For that reason alone I've never allowed Le Corbusier to make my acquaintance.

—Frank Lloyd Wright

OSCAR LEVANT

Pearl is a disease of oysters. Levant is a disease of Hollywood.

—Kenneth Tynan

. . . a man who, if he did not exist, could not be imagined.

—S. N. Behrman

Sinclair Lewis

He seems to join in about equal parts the
bonehead, the sorehead, and the solemn ass.
—James Gould Cozzens

Wyndham Lewis

I do not think I have ever seen a nastier-
looking man. Some people show evil as a
great racehorse shows breeding. They have
the dignity of a hard *chancre*. Lewis did not
show evil; he just looked nasty.
—Ernest Hemingway

Liberace

This deadly, winking, sniggering, snuggling,
scent-impregnated, chromium-plated, lumi-
nous, quivering, giggling, fruit-flavored,
mincing, ice-covered heap of mother-
love . . .
—William Connor

President Abraham Lincoln

This man's appearance, his pedigree, his coarse low jokes and anecdotes, his vulgar smiles and his frivolity, are a disgrace to the seat he holds. . . .

—John Wilkes Booth

His mind works in the right directions but seldom works clearly and cleanly. His bread is of unbolted flour, and much straw, too, mixes in the bran, and sometimes gravel stones.

—Henry Ward Beecher

JOHN V. LINDSAY, CITY MAYOR OF NEW YORK

He thinks like Nixon, talks like Eisenhower, goofs like Goldwater.

—Noel Parmentel

DAVID LLOYD GEORGE

My one ardent desire is that after the war he should be publicly castrated in front of Nurse Cavell's statue.

—Lytton Strachey

VINCE LOMBARDI

He's fair. He treats us all the same—like dogs.

—Henry Jordan
(of the Green Bay Packers, 1970)

KING LOUIS XVI AND QUEEN MARIE ANTOINETTE

What is there in the delivering over of a perjured blockhead and an unprincipled prostitute into the hands of the hangman, that it should arrest for a moment attention?

—Robert Burns
(on their execution)

IDA LUPINO

Her familiar expression of strained intensity would be less quickly relieved by a merciful death than by Ex-Lax.

—James Agee

DOUGLAS MACARTHUR

I fired MacArthur because he wouldn't respect the authority of the president. I didn't fire him because he was a dumb son of a bitch, although he was.

—President Harry S Truman

Oh yes, I studied dramatics under him for twelve years.

—President Dwight Eisenhower

Never trust a man who combs his hair straight from his left armpit.

—Alice Roosevelt Longworth

THOMAS BABINGTON MACAULAY

He has occasional flashes of silence that make his conversation perfectly delightful.

—Reverend Sydney Smith

SENATOR JOSEPH R. McCARTHY

. . . a putrescent and scabious object that is obnoxious to the senses of sight, smell, and hearing—a thing obscene and loathesome, and not to be touched except with sterilized fire tongs.

—Harold L. Ickes

. . . a ballyhoo artist who has to cover up his shortcomings by wild charges.

—President Harry S Truman

MARY MCCARTHY

When Mary stroked your arm, that was real blood that came out.

—Eileen Simpson

HUGH MACDIARMID, SCOTTISH POET

. . . is there any bit [of his work] that's notably less morally repugnant and aesthetically null than the rest?

—Philip Larkin

JEANETTE MACDONALD and NELSON EDDY

I had forgotten the insane coquetting of Miss Jeanette MacDonald allied to a triumphant lack of acting ability. I had forgotten the resolute, stocky flabby heaviness of Mr. Nelson Eddy.

—Sir Noel Coward
(of the film *Bitter Sweet*)

PRESIDENT WILLIAM MCKINLEY

Why, if a man were to call my dog McKinley and the brute failed to resent to the death the damning insult, I'd drown it.
—William Cowper Brann

HAROLD MACMILLAN

Every time Mr. Macmillan comes back from abroad, Mr. Butler goes to the airport and grips him warmly by the throat.
—Harold Wilson

MADONNA

Ms. Grotesque Personified
—Michael M. Thomas

ETHEL MANNIN

I do not want Miss Mannin's feelings to be hurt by the fact that I have never heard of her. . . . At the moment I am debarred from the pleasure of putting her in her place by the fact that she has not got one.
—Dame Edith Sitwell

GROUCHO MARX

The most embarrassingly unfunny comedian I have ever encountered.

—Kingsley Amis

MARY, QUEEN OF SCOTS

. . . The most notorious whore in all the world.

—Peter Wentworth

A. E. MATTHEWS

A. E. Matthews ambled through *This Was a Man* like a charming retriever who has buried a bone and can't quite remember where.

—Sir Noel Coward

W. SOMERSET MAUGHAM

Willie Maugham came in: like a dead man whose beard or moustache has grown a little grisly after death. And his lips are drawn back like a ded mans. He has small ferret eyes. A look of suffering & malignity & meanness & suspicion. A mechanical voice as if he had to raise a lever at each word—stiffens talk into something hard cut measured.

—Virginia Woolf

That old lady is a crashing bore.

—Dorothy Parker

ELSA MAXWELL, SOCIETY AND POLITICAL HOSTESS

She was built for crowds. She never came any closer to life than the dinner table.

—Genet (Janet Flanner)

I once took her to a masquerade party . . . at the stroke of midnight, I ripped off her mask and discovered I had beheaded her!

Oscar Levant

GEORGE MEREDITH and ROBERT BROWNING

Meredith is a prose Browning, and so is Browning. He used poetry as a medium for writing in prose.

—Oscar Wilde

EDNA ST. VINCENT MILLAY

. . . the career of Edna Millay presented the still sadder spectacle of a poet who withered on the stalk before attaining fruition.

—George F. Whitcher

KATE MILLETT, AMERICAN WOMEN'S LIBERATION CHAMPION

American feminism began when Kate Millett, that imploding beanbag of poisonous self-pity, declared Freud a sexist.

—Camille Paglia

LIZA MINELLI

I always thought Miss Minelli's face deserving—of first prize in a beagle category.

—John Simon

JOHN MITCHELL, U.S. ATTORNEY GENERAL, NIXON ADMINISTRATION

. . . there was something turnipy about him . . . he had small lifeless eyes like those of a wintering potato.

—Mary McCarthy

GEORGE MOORE

. . . a man carved from a turnip, looking out of astonished eyes.

—William Butler Yeats

That old yahoo George Moore. . . . His stories impressed me as being on the whole like gruel spooned up off a dirty floor.

—Jane Barlow

THOMAS MOORE

Mr. Moore converts the wild harp of Erin into a musical snuffbox.

—William Hazlitt

HENRY MORGENTHAU

Morgenthau didn't know shit from apple butter.

—President Harry S Truman

FRANK A. MUNSEY, AMERICAN NEWSPAPER PUBLISHER

The talent of a meat-packer, the morals of a moneychanger, and the manners of an undertaker.

—William Allen White

RUPERT MURDOCH

He debauched our culture and corrupted our youth, producing a generation of lager louts, sex maniacs, and morons.

—Francis Wheen

VLADIMIR NABOKOV

[His works] in general secrete as much milk of kindness as a cornered black mamba.

—Ronald Hingley

ANAÏS NIN

Nin's tendencies as a writer toward garrulous self-absorption and florid self-dramatization feel heightened in this volume, as she gushes on and on about her sexual relationships, endowing them with nearly metaphysical importance . . .

—Michiko Kakutani
(reviewing *Incest* in *New York Times*)

PRESIDENT RICHARD M. NIXON

Mr. Nixon may be very good in kitchen debates, but so are a great many other married men I know.

Last Thursday night Mr. Nixon dismissed me as "another Truman." I regard this as a compliment. I consider him another Dewey.
—President John F. Kennedy

President Nixon's motto was: If two wrongs don't make a right, try three.
—Norman Cousins

The real Nixon was a pathetic, fearful man who spent his life prophesying his own failures and living up to his own prophecies.
—Joseph Heller

The only dope worth shooting is Richard Nixon.
—Abbie Hoffman

. . . a monument to all the rancid genes and broken chromosomes that corrupt the possibilities of the American Dream.
—Hunter S. Thompson

Presidents Richard M. Nixon, Gerald Ford, James Earl Carter, Ronald Reagan

Nixon, Ford, Carter, Reagan—a Mount Rushmore of incompetence.

—David Steinberg

Alfred Nobel

I can forgive Alfred Nobel for having invented dynamite, but only a fiend in human form could have invented the Nobel Prize.

—George Bernard Shaw

Merle Oberon

She was very strange-looking. I could not connect this woman who looked somewhat mummified and pickled in brine with the beautiful young wild Cathy of *Wuthering Heights*.

—Carol Matthau

DANIEL O'CONNELL

The only way to deal with such a man as O'Connell is to hang him up and erect a statue to him under the gallows.

—Reverend Sydney Smith

CLIFFORD ODETS

Odets, where is thy sting?

—George S. Kaufman

FRANK O'HARA, AND THE "NEW YORK SCHOOL" OF POETS

What I marvel at when I read an O'Hara poem, or any other New York School poem, is the incredibly high marks they seem to award themselves just for picking up their pens. It's as if they had been set down in front of the finger paints by adoring mothers who can hardly wait to frame their darling's doodles.

—Hugo Williams

LAURENCE OLIVIER

Compared to the ordinary man with ordinary ambitions Larry was a deep-sea monster.

—Peter Glenville
(English director)

YOKO ONO

Her voice sounded like an eagle being goosed.

—Ralph Novak

A. R. ORAGE, ENGLISH EDITOR AND MYSTIC

. . . a very hotbed of culture, you could grow mushrooms on him.

—James Stephens

P. J. O'Rourke

. . . "Mencken," they style this witless homunculus . . . the kind of ignorant pinheaded loudmouth political pimp Mencken boned and gutted for breakfast.

—Tony Hendra

Paul Osborn

Perhaps his most memorable work, which places him as a writer, was his 1950s stage adaptation of the novel, *The World of Suzie Wong*, which became known around New York as "The World of Woozy Song."

—Richard Hornby

Wilfred Owen

. . . there's every excuse for him, but no excuse for those who liked him.

—William Butler Yeats

He is all blood, dirt, and sucked sugar stick.

—William Butler Yeats

Reverend Ian Paisley

Paisley might not convert an atheist to a belief in God but he certainly had me converted to a belief in the devil.

—Dervla Murphy

Hughes Panassié, French jazz critic

Who does that Frog think he is to come over here and try to tell us how to play? We don't go over there and tell them how to jump on a grape.

—Eddie Condon

Norman Vincent Peale

I find Paul appealing and Peale appalling.

—Adlai E. Stevenson

Drew Pearson

He is only a filthy-brain child, conceived in ruthlessness and dedicated to the proposition that Judas Iscariot was a piker.

—Senator William Jenner

H. Ross Perot

You can't compete with a pet rock.

—Dee Dee Myers
(press secretary to Bill Clinton)

The teeny-weeny Mussolini from Texas.

—Tony Hendra

. . . he had a face like a Toby jug and a voice like Frank Perdue.

—Russell Baker

They looked at him and saw a hand grenade with a bad haircut.

—Peggy Noonan

General John J. Pershing

Rumors of peace talks worried him. Peace would ruin his plans for an American army.

—John Dos Passos

KING PHILIP II OF SPAIN

I cannot find it in me to fear a man who
took ten years a-learning his alphabet.
—Queen Elizabeth I of England
(1533–1603)

GIFFORD PINCHOT, GOVERNOR OF PENNSYLVANIA

. . . a piscatorial politician . . . a persistent
fisherman in political waters, who exempli-
fies more than anyone else in American
public life how the itch for public office can
break down one's intellectual integrity.
—Harold L. Ickes

NORMAN PODHORETZ, AMERICAN MAGAZINE EDITOR

[a] moral and intellectual hooligan who
wishes he had the balls to be a real-life rat
fink.

—Christopher Hitchens

EDGAR ALLAN POE

The Jingle Man.

—Ralph Waldo Emerson

ALEXANDER POPE

He hardly drank tea without a strategem.

—Samuel Johnson

I wonder that he is not thrashed; but his littleness is his protection, no man shoots a wren.

—William Broome

COLE PORTER

He sang like a hinge.

—Ethel Merman

EZRA POUND

He is blatant, full of foolish archaisms, obscure through awkward language, not subtle thought, and formless.

—Rupert Brooke
(on Pound's poems)

. . . a village explainer, excellent if you were a village, but if you were not, not.

—Gertrude Stein

He never acknowledges anything as good unless he, *der grosser Ich,* has had a hand in bringing it to the world's attention. I have been frequently nauseated by his pretensions.

—William Carlos Williams

ANTHONY POWELL

. . . a horse-faced dwarf.

—Philip Larkin

OTTO PREMINGER

He's really Martin Bormann in elevator shoes, with a face-lift by a blindfolded plastic surgeon in Luxembourg.

—Billy Wilder

ELVIS PRESLEY

By now, little resemblance could be seen to the marvelous young punk who had revolutionized the posture, intonation, and wet dreams of postwar British youth. In 1976, just a year before his death from narcotics abuse, he was a walking mummy, encrusted with seventies tomb-ornaments, obese, incontinent, and almost blind.

—Philip Norman

DAN QUAYLE, AMERICAN VICE PRESIDENT

I realized that to think about Dan Quayle as much as I have is beginning to affect my brain.

—Deborah Werksman
(coeditor of "The Quayle Quarterly,"
on its demise)

If a tree fell in a forest, and no one was there to hear it, it might sound like Dan Quayle looks.

—Tom Shales

"I just know he has the smallest penis. I mean we're talking freezing-cold acorns in his pants, screaming, *screaming* for cover.

—Carrie Fisher
(author and actress)

Dan Quayle is more stupid than Ronald Reagan put together!

—Matt Groening
(creator of *The Simpsons*)

He's like Redford's retarded brother that they kept up in the attic, and he got out somehow.

—Patti Marx
(writer)

Dan Quayle is the penumbra that hangs over the end of the twentieth century. Is there anything in Revelations about a blond mental defective bringing about the end of the world?

—Dr. Kerry K. Willis

I don't want to be charged with child abuse.
                              —Patrick Buchanan
              (when he was asked why he did not
                  answer Quayle's charges that he
                      was not fit to be president)

AYN RAND

. . . she really was a cracked pot, though of a noble sort. . . . To gather with her New York adherents . . . is a disquieting experience. I have rarely seen so many unattractive malcontents in one place at one time.
                              —Hiram Haydn

PRESIDENT RONALD REAGAN

He is a true velvet fascist, really smooth.
                              —Shirley MacLaine

I've got this hearing aid. Ronnie Reagan has two. Of course, there's nothing in between his.

                              —Studs Terkel

You could argue that you should never con-
fuse real life and politics or you will begin
to believe things that Ronald Reagan says.

—Anna Quindlen

Washington couldn't tell a lie, Nixon
couldn't tell the truth, and Reagan couldn't
tell the difference.

—Mort Sahl

So shockingly dumb that by his very presence
in the office he numbs an entire country.

—Jimmy Breslin

If you think of Harry Truman's adage: "The
buck stops here," Reagan's version would
be: "The buck? I never even saw the buck.
Let me know when it comes into the room."

—Stanley Bing

ROBERT REDFORD

Poor little man. They made him out of
lemon Jello-O and there he is.

—Adela Rogers Saint John

CECIL RHODES

I admire him, I frankly confess it; and when his time comes I shall buy a piece of the rope for a keepsake.

—Mark Twain

SENATOR ABRAHAM RIBICOFF

You motherfucking Jew bastard, get your ass out of Chicago.

Richard E. Daley

RALPH RICHARDSON

The glass eye in the forehead of English acting.

—Kenneth Tynan

ADMIRAL HYMAN GEORGE RICKOVER

A final malady that afflicted—and continues to afflict—the whole navy, though the surface navy was and is the greatest sufferer, can be described in one word: Rickover.

—Elmo R. Zumwalt

Leni Riefenstahl, cinematographer, friend of Hitler

Riefenstahl's thirst for applause, her bottomless narcissism, is worse than tedious, she is so dazzled by her own light that she notices nothing, but nothing, around her.

—Ian Buruma

Diana Rigg

Diana Rigg is built like a brick mausoleum with insufficient flying buttresses.

—John Simon

James Whitcomb Riley

... the unctuous, over-cheerful, word-mouthing, flabby-faced citizen who condescendingly tells Providence, in flowery and well-rounded periods, where to get off.

—Hewlett Howland

LORD PATRICK ROBERTSON

Here lies that peerless paper peer Lord Peter
Who broke the laws of God and man and
meter.

—Sir Walter Scott

PRESIDENT THEODORE ROOSEVELT

When Theodore attends a wedding he
wants to be the bride and when he attends
a funeral he wants to be the corpse.

—one of Roosevelt's relatives

LORD ROSEBERRY

A man who never missed an occasion to let
slip an opportunity.

—George Bernard Shaw

HAROLD ROSS, EDITOR OF THE *NEW YORKER*

He looks like a dishonest Abe Lincoln.

—Alexander Woollcott

MICKEY ROURKE

[Rourke] had been riding a motorcycle without a helmet for far too long. And he's punch-drunk from being in the ring.

—Spike Lee

JEAN JACQUES ROUSSEAU

He melts with tenderness for those who only touch him by the remotest relation and then, without one natural pang, casts away as a sort of offal and excrement, the spawn of his disgustful amours.

The bear loves, licks, and forms her young but bears are not philosophers.

—Edmund Burke

DAMON RUNYON

Damon will throw a drowning man both ends of the rope.

—anonymous acquaintance

BERTRAND RUSSELL

The enemy of all mankind, you are, full of the lust of enmity. It is *not* the hatred of falsehood which inspires you. It is the hatred of people, of flesh and blood. It is a perverted blood-lust. Why don't you own it?

—D. H. Lawrence

CAMILLE SAINT-SÄENS

If he'd been making shell cases during the war it might have been better for music.

—Maurice Ravel

GEORGE SAND

A great cow full of ink.

—Gustav Flaubert

CARL SANDBURG

The cruellest thing that has happened to Lincoln since he was shot by Booth has been to fall into the hands of Carl Sandburg.

—Edmund Wilson
(on Sandburg's biography of Abraham Lincoln)

GEORGE SANTAYANA

He stood on the flat road to heaven and buttered slides to hell for all the rest.

—Oliver Wendell Holmes

GENERAL WINFIELD SCOTT

He understands nothing, appreciates nothing, and is ever in my way.

—George B. McClellan

William Shakespeare

I think that Shakespeare is a shit. Absolute shit! He may have been a genius for his time, but I just can't relate to that stuff. "Thee and thous"—the guy sounds like a faggot.

—Gene Simmons
(of Kiss)

He is the very Janus of poets; he wears, almost everywhere, two faces: and you have scarce begun to admire the one, e'er you despise the other.

—John Dryden

George Bernard Shaw

One might still be hopeful for Mr. Shaw's future as a dramatist, despite his present incompetence, if there were any hint in his plays of creative power. But there is no such hint.

—Arnold Bennett

. . . a man without conscience, though that was a common enough failing, but the only man I have ever known without a heart.

—Bertrand Russell

Mr. Shaw is (I suspect) the only man on earth who has never written any poetry.

—G. K. Chesterton

PERCY BYSSHE SHELLEY

Poor Shelley always was, and is, a kind of ghastly object; colorless, pallid, tuneless, without health or warmth or vigor.

—Thomas Carlyle

He was a liar and a cheat; he paid no regard to truth, nor to any kind of moral obligation.

—Robert Southey

Upton Sinclair, American novelist who ran for Governor of California

. . . an incurable romantic, wholesale believer in the obviously not so. The man delights me constantly . . . I know of no one in all this vast paradise of credulity who gives a steadier and more heroic credit to the intrinsically preposterous.

—H. L. Mencken

Edith Sitwell

Then Edith Sitwell appeared, her nose longer than an anteater's, and read some of her absurd stuff.

—Lytton Strachey

So you've been reviewing Edith Sitwell's latest piece of virgin dung, have you? Isn't she a poisonous thing of a woman, lying, concealing, flipping, plagiarizing, misquoting, and being as clever a crooked literary publicist as ever.

—Dylan Thomas

... stupidity ... is, after all, the most obvious characteristic of this writer; she was in everything she wrote an amateur, a poseur of art. Frequently she has to break off ... to instruct her servile readers in the virtues, not of poetry, but of her poetry, servile once more to herself.

—Geoffrey Grigson

DAME ETHEL SMYTH, BRITISH COMPOSER

She would be like Richard Wagner if only she looked a bit more feminine.

—Osbert Sitwell

ALEXANDER SOLZHENITSYN

It is sad that the dumb Swedes gave their merit badge to Solzhenitsyn instead of Nabokov. ... The Russians displayed uncharacteristic humor in letting this nut come to our shores.

—Gore Vidal

He is a bad novelist and a fool. The combination usually makes for great popularity in the U.S.

—Gore Vidal

JOSEPH STALIN

A little bit of a squirt.

—President Harry S Truman

RICHARD STEELE

Steele might become a reasonably good writer if he would pay a little attention to grammar, learn something about the propriety and disposition of words and, incidentally, get some information on the subject he intends to handle.

—Jonathan Swift
(attributed)

GERTRUDE STEIN

Shall we ever discover anything piquant about Gertrude Stein? As, for example, that she has been all these many years just a humorist quietly enjoying herself at our expense?

—Vincent Starrett

. . . the cold suet roll . . . was . . . the same sticky opaque mass all through and all along . . . weighted and projected with a sibylline urge . . . mournful and monstrous, fat without nerve.

—Wyndham Lewis

. . . a tub of old guts.

—Ezra Pound

Reading Gertrude Stein at length is not unlike making one's way through an interminable and badly printed game book.

—Richard Briegeman

What an old covered wagon, she is.

—F. Scott Fitzgerald

She got to look like a Roman emperor and that was fine if you liked your women to look like Roman emperors.

—Ernest Hemingway

JOHN STEINBECK

I can't read ten pages of Steinbeck without throwing up.

—James Gould Cozzens

ADLAI STEVENSON

Adlai Stevenson was a man who could never make up his mind whether he had to go to the bathroom or not.

—President Harry S Truman

ROD STEWART

Rod Stewart has an attractive voice and a highly unattractive bottom. . . . He now spends more time wagging the latter than exercising the former.

—Clive James

RICHARD STRAUSS

Such an astounding lack of talent was never before united to such pretentiousness.

—Peter Ilyich Tchaikovsky

BARBRA STREISAND

Miss Streisand looks like a cross between an aardvark and an albino rat surmounted by a platinum-coated horse bun.

—John Simon

SENATOR CHARLES SUMNER

He identifies himself so completely with the universe that he is not at all certain whether he is part of the universe or the universe is part of him. He is a reviser of the decalogue. You will soon see the Sermon on the Mount revised, corrected, and greatly enlarged and improved by Senator Sumner.

—Matthew Carpenter

Jonathan Swift

A monster gibbering, shrieking, and gnashing imprecations against mankind.

—William Makepeace Thackeray

Algernon Swinburne

. . . a perpetual functioning of genius without truth, feeling, or any adequate matter to be functioning on.

—Gerard Manley Hopkins

ELIZABETH TAYLOR

Let's face it, Elizabeth Taylor's last marriage was all about selling perfume because it's hard to sell perfume when you're a fat old spinster.

—Johnny Rotten

RENATA TEBALDI

Miss Renata Tebaldi was always sweet and very firm . . . she had dimples of iron.

—Rudolf Bing

ALFRED, LORD TENNYSON

Let school-miss Alfred vent her chaste delight On darling little rooms so warm and bright.

—Edward Bulwer-Lytton

Tennyson is a beautiful half of a poet.

—Ralph Waldo Emerson

He had a large, loose-limbed body, a swarthy complexion, a high, narrow forehead, and huge bricklayer's hands; in youth he looked like a gypsy; in age like a dirty old monk; he had the finest ear, perhaps, of any English poet; he was also undoubtedly the stupidest; there was little about melancholia that he didn't know; there was little else that he did.

—W. H. Auden

MARGARET THATCHER

Mrs. Thatcher is doing for monetarism what the Boston Strangler did for door-to-door salesmen.

—Denis Healey

I cannot bring myself to vote for a woman who has been voice-trained to speak to me as though my dog has just died.

—Keith Waterhouse

DYLAN THOMAS

Who cares if this poet sozzled, or made a public dive at parties for the more appetizingly outlined, if still virginal breasts? (The answer to that rhetorical question, I am afraid, is that many Americans do care, in a *frisson* of excitement over the antics of genius.)

—Geoffrey Grigson

He was a detestable man. Men pressed money on him, and women their bodies. Dylan took both with equal contempt. His great pleasure was to humiliate people.

—A. J. P. Taylor

. . . a demagogic masturbator.

—Robert Graves

. . . an overgrown baby.

—Truman Capote

A pernicious figure, one who has helped to get Wales and Welsh poetry a bad name and . . . done lasting harm to both.

—Kingsley Amis

R. S. Thomas, Welsh poet and clergyman

... not noticeably Welsh, which is one comfort.

—Philip Larkin

Anthony Trollope

He has a gross and repulsive face and manner, but appears *bon enfant* when you talk with him. But he is the dullest Briton of them all.

—Henry James

President Harry S Truman

You can't make a president out of a ribbon clerk.

—Al Whitney

... the *reductio ad absurdum* of the common man.

—Henry R. Luce

DONALD TRUMP

The reason they're giving for the divorce is that Donald has been having a long-term affair with himself.

—Arsenio Hall

PRESIDENT JOHN TYLER

He has been called a mediocre man; but this is an unwarranted flattery. He was a politician of monumental littleness.

—President Theodore Roosevelt

KENNETH TYNAN

Kenneth Tynan read the autocue as if it contained a threatening letter from somebody else instead of a script written by himself.

—Clive James

QUEEN VICTORIA

Nowadays, a parlor maid as ignorant as Queen Victoria was when she came to the throne would be classed as mentally defective.

—George Bernard Shaw

Queen Victoria was like a great paperweight that for half a century sat upon men's minds, and when she was removed their ideas began to blow all over the place haphazardly.

—H. G. Wells

GORE VIDAL

Anyone who lies about Mr. Vidal is doing him a kindness.

—William F. Buckley, Jr.

JON VOIGHT, AMERICAN SCREEN ACTOR

The actor has been in the movies for so long that, as we can tell from his blinking, befogged look, he can't believe he is not on a soundstage. He acts in the low-keyed, low-grade way of someone confident that his performance will be spliced together in the editing room.

—John Simon
(of Voight on stage)

VOLTAIRE

The godless arch-scoundrel Voltaire is dead—dead like a dog, like a beast.

—Wolfgang Amadeus Mozart

PAUL VON HINDENBURG

Here the general slept before the battle of Tannenberg; here also the general slept after the battle; and between you and me, during the battle too.

—Max Hoffman

JOACHIM VON RIBBENTROP

Bought his name, married his money, and cheated himself into his job.

—Joseph Goebbels

[There could be] no hell in Dante's inferno bad enough for him.

—Sir Neville Henderson

RICHARD WAGNER

I like Wagner's music better than any other music. It is so loud that one can talk the whole time without people hearing what one says. That is a great advantage.

—Oscar Wilde

I love Wagner, but the music I prefer is that of a cat hung up by its tail outside a window and trying to stick to the panes of glass with its claws.

—Charles Baudelaire

GEORGE WALLACE

I don't think you'll have to worry that this mental midget, this hillbilly Hitler from Alabama, is anywhere near becoming the nominee of the Democratic party.

—Julian Bond

Governor Wallace was supposed to be here, but I understand he couldn't make it. It seems he is busy conferring with Alabama's leading mathematicians, geologists, and physicists. They're preparing a new simple literacy test for the voters of Selma!

—Hubert Humphrey

HENRY A. WALLACE, AMERICAN VICE PRESIDENT

. . . one of the most thumping asses ever heard of in American politics.

—H. L. Mencken

Much of what Mr. Wallace calls his global thinking is, no matter how you slice it, still Globaloney.

—Clare Booth Luce

HUGH WALPOLE

No other age can have produced such a manikin of letters. He is the impact of commerce, or rather advertisement, upon belles lettres.

—E. M. Forster

ISAAK WALTON

The quaint old cruel coxcomb, in his gullet
Should have a hook and a small trout to pull it.
— George Gordon, Lord Byron
(in *Don Juan*)

ANDY WARHOL

He's a sphinx without a secret.
— Truman Capote

PRESIDENT GEORGE WASHINGTON

As to you, sir, treacherous to private friendship (for so you have been to me, and that in the day of danger) and a hypocrite in public life, the world will be puzzled to decide whether you are an apostate or an imposter, whether you have abandoned good principles or whether you ever had any.

—Thomas Paine
(letter to Washington, July 30, 1796)

That dark designing sordid ambitious vain proud arrogant and vindictive knave.

—Charles Lee

EVELYN WAUGH

Did *you* get the treatment? That mushroomy paw dropping yours before you've had a chance to shake it? Little eyes fixed on the ceiling when you try to talk?

—Truman Capote

Horrible little man. What I couldn't bear about him was the way he arse-crept rich and important people. . . . Little fart. You know I used to be Lady something. Nobody could have made more fuss about me while I was. And nobody could have started ignoring me quicker when I stopped being it.

—Marilyn Quennell

ANDREW LLOYD WEBBER

I find Mr. Lloyd Webber's phenomenal success one of the great mysteries of modern times. I have listened to many of his tunes and never once heard one that I wanted to hear again.

—Richard Ingrams

Andrew Lloyd Webber has done for music what Bomber Harris did for landscape gardening.

—Miles Kington

RAQUEL WELCH

She's one of the few actresses in Hollywood history who looks more animated in still photographs than she does on the screen.

—Michael Medved

H. G. WELLS

The Old Maid among novelists; even the sex obsession that lay clotted on Ann Veronica and The New Machiavelli like cold white sauce was merely Old Maid's mania.

—Rebecca West

FRANZ WERFEL

He has once again shrunk to the small hateful, corpulent Jew—my first impression.

—Alma Mahler-Werfel
(after years of marriage)

JAMES WHISTLER

I have never seen, and heard, much of cockney impudence before now, but never expected to hear a coxcomb ask two hundred guineas for flinging a pot of paint in the public's face.

—John Ruskin

PATRICK WHITE, AUSTRALIAN NOBEL PRIZE–WINNING WRITER

He was truly an unpleasant character: moody, arrogant, spiteful, incapable of forgiveness. He yelled at dinner-party guests; exploded in rage at friends; snubbed people publicly.

—Andrew Sullivan

WALT WHITMAN

Mr. Whitman's muse is at once indecent and ugly, lascivious and gawky, lubricious and coarse.

—Lafcadio Hearn

A large shaggy dog, just unchained, scouring the beaches of the world and baying at the moon.

—Robert Louis Stevenson

OSCAR WILDE

He festooned the dung heap on which he had placed himself with sonnets as people grow honeysuckle around outdoor privies.

—Quentin Crisp

KING WILLIAM IV OF ENGLAND

King William blew his nose twice, and wiped the royal perspiration from a face which is probably the largest uncivilized spot in England.

—Oliver Wendell Holmes

ESTHER WILLIAMS

Wet she's a star—dry she ain't.

—Fanny Brice
(sometimes attributed to Joseph Pasternak)

TENNESSEE WILLIAMS

I am disappointed in my continued disappointment in Williams. And I am afraid I am doomed to keep on being disappointed in him until either I enter my second childhood or he outgrows his first.

—George Jean Nathan

GARRY WILLS

As usual, to put it politely, Garry Wills erases the distinction between reporting and creative writing.

—Jeffrey Hart

A. N. WILSON, ENGLISH NOVELIST AND BIOGRAPHER

. . . a remnant of sick on the pavement would be too great, too substantial a description of the man.

—Lady Lucinda Lambton

HAROLD WILSON

... he did not (as one had charitably or ignorantly assumed) betray his principles or abandon his beliefs under pressure or from self-interest: he just had no principles or beliefs to abandon or betray. The U-turn is Harold's normal mode of progression; it is as natural to him as it is to a crab to walk sideways.

—Enoch Powell

PRESIDENT WOODROW WILSON

How can I talk to a fellow who thinks himself the first man in two thousand years to know anything about peace on earth?

—Georges Clemenceau

While God required only Ten Commandments, Wilson needed fourteen.

—Georges Clemenceau

THE DUKE AND DUCHESS OF WINDSOR

. . . a life of exile and idleness, nightclubs and boredom—a dutiful playboy, a greedy woman who charged for their appearance at parties, a thousand dollars for ten minutes.

—Helen Bevington

P. G. WODEHOUSE

English Literature's performing flea.

—Sean O'Casey

THOMAS WOLFE

He was the greatest five-year-old that ever lived.

—Norman Mailer

Anybody that admires Thomas Wolfe can be expected to like good fiction only by accident.

—Flannery O'Connor

If it must be Thomas, let it be Mann, and if it must be Wolfe let it be Nero, but never let it be Thomas Wolfe.

—Peter De Vries

VIRGINIA WOOLF

I enjoyed talking to her, but thought nothing of her writing. I considered her "a beautiful little knitter."

—Dame Edith Sitwell

ALEXANDER WOOLLCOTT

. . . a fat duchess with the emotions of a fish.

—Harold Ross

. . . here is a partial list of the nicknames by which A. Woollcott was called, at one time or another: Cream Puff, First Grave Digger, der Führer, Gila monster, God's big brother, Ilex, Louisa M. Alcott, Old Untouchable, Putt, Putrid, Seidlitz Powder, Slimer, Stentor.

—Vincent Starrett

WILLIAM WORDSWORTH

The languid way in which he gives you a handful of numb unresponsive fingers is very significant.

—Thomas Carlyle

WILLIAM BUTLER YEATS

. . . though he could at times be very good company, he was a pompous, vain man; to hear him read his own verses was as excruciating a torture as anyone could be exposed to.

—W. Somerset Maugham

. . . a detestable poetaster.

—Robert Graves

[Looks like] an umbrella left behind at a picnic.

—George Moore

Morton Zuckerman, American real estate millionaire and magazine owner

I tailored Fred Allen's characterization of Hollywood to fit Mr. Zuckerman: "All of his integrity would fit into the navel of a flea. And there'd be room left over for a caraway seed and his heart."

—Robert Manning
(editor, *The Atlantic*)

He has the ethical sense of a pack of jackals.
—Gloria Steinem

INDEX

Personal names appearing in plain type indicate the source of the quotation and those in capitals indicate the person who is the subject of the quotation.